When the Sun Comes Out After Three Days of Rain

When the Sun Comes Out After Three Days of Rain

Poems by

Leah Browning

© 2022 Leah Browning. All rights reserved.
This material may not be reproduced in any form, published,
reprinted, recorded, performed, broadcast,
rewritten or redistributed without
the explicit permission of Leah Browning.
All such actions are strictly prohibited by law.

Cover design by Shay Culligan
Cover photograph by Alexander
Cover sculpture by Walter Moroder

ISBN: 978-1-63980-217-3

Kelsay Books
502 South 1040 East, A-119
American Fork, Utah 84003
Kelsaybooks.com

For my family

Acknowledgments

Grateful acknowledgment is made to the editors of the following publications in which these poems first appeared, sometimes in slightly different form:

All Things Girl: "Spring Arrives Late"
Amygdala: "The Blue Room," "Crossing from One Continent to the Next," "Time Loops Back on Itself"
Autumn Sky Poetry Daily: "Paris"
Belletrist Magazine: "Probabilities"
The Broadkill Review: "American Housewife," "Suburban Dreams"
Clementine Unbound: "Charley Horse"
Coldnoon: "Approaching the Intersection of Princess and Bath"
Corium Magazine: "More Than 1,000 Dead Birds Fall from the Sky in Arkansas"
Dressing Room Poetry Journal: "Any Day Now"
Eunoia Review: "In the Chair Museum," "The Night He Broke His Collarbone," "On the Way Back to the Museum"
Extract(s): "There's Nothing"
Freshwater Literary Journal: "In the Meadow Next to the Rented House," "In Transit"
Glassworks Magazine: "The First Day You Were in the Psychiatric Hospital"
Lighthouse Weekly: "Encyclopedia Britannica," "5150"
Lily: "April in Minnesota"
The Literary Bohemian: "A Common Language," "Dinner with Mohamoud," "Refrain"
Mud Season Review: "Visiting Hours"
Mulberry Literary: "Imperial Butterfly House, Vienna"
Poetry South: "Vancouver-Beijing"
Queen's Feminist Review: "Instincts"
Queen's Quarterly: "Damage"
Scapegoat Review: "In the Valley"
The Stillwater Review: "Peripheral Vision"

Sybil Journal: "Texas"
Tipton Poetry Journal: "Looking for What Is Lost," "Velocity"
White Whale Review: "A White Boat on a Blue, Blue Sea"
8-West Press: "Time Zones"

"Learning to Play Piano at Thirty" first appeared on a series of postcards from the program Poetry Jumps Off the Shelf.

Some of the poems included in this collection were previously published in the following chapbooks by Leah Browning:

Making Love to the Same Man for Fifteen Years (Big Table Publishing, 2009)
Picking Cherries in the Española Valley (Dancing Girl Press, 2010)
In the Chair Museum (Dancing Girl Press, 2013)
Out of Body (Dancing Girl Press, 2018)

Contents

In the Chair Museum	13
Approaching the Intersection of Princess and Bath	15
Crossing the Border	16
Charley Horse	19
Peripheral Vision	21
Horseshoe Falls	22
Vancouver-Beijing	24
Any Day Now	26
Milk (1983)	28
March 1, 2012	30
The Most Fragile Part of the Human Body	32
Take a Seat	35
Lucky Stars	37
There's Nothing	39
On the Way Back to the Museum	40
Dinner with Mohamoud	41
The Night He Broke His Collarbone	42
Blue	45
Time Zones	46
Mid-Week	48
When the Sun Comes Out After Three Days of Rain	49
I Wrapped My Dishes in Newsprint	50
In Transit	52
Imperial Butterfly House, Vienna	53
The First Day You Were in the Psychiatric Hospital	54
Crossing from One Continent to the Next	55
Visiting Hours	57
The Blue Room	58
Driving Alone at Night on an Unfamiliar Highway (November)	60
Time Loops Back on Itself	61
Paris	62

Cutting	64
Problems (#1)	65
Problems (#2)	66
Calling 911	67
Spring Arrives Late	68
Almost a Year After His Suicide	69
Encyclopedia Britannica	70
More Than 1,000 Dead Birds Fall from the Sky in Arkansas	71
A Common Language	73
Damage	74
American Housewife	76
Suburban Dreams	78
A Cupboard Full of Keys	81
Open the Door	83
Wednesday Afternoon	84
In the Valley	86
Texas	88
We Argue About the Aesthetics of Garbage	89
Instincts	90
Refrain	92
Looking for What Is Lost	93
A White Boat on a Blue, Blue Sea	95
Learning to Play Piano at Thirty	96
April in Minnesota	97
At Last, I Am Returned	99
In the Driveway, Washing the Car	100
Probabilities	102
Velocity	103
5150	104
Late May, Botanic Garden, Santa Barbara	108
In the Meadow Next to the Rented House	109

In the Chair Museum

On Christmas Day, we drove north
to spend the afternoon with friends.

I was homesick for New Mexico
and brought biscochitos in the shape of stars.

We all walked to Montara State Beach
where it was cold and windy and beautiful

and watched the sun set like a piece of golden glass
over the ocean. I couldn't believe it was truly

December. On the way back to the house
I held his little mitten in my gloved hand.

He was getting older and it felt like the last time
this might happen, like I needed to remember it.

We took the longest route and stopped to look
at strings of Christmas lights in the front yards.

By the time we returned, the men had built
a fire in a metal bowl on the back porch.

Later, after dinner, I looked through a book
with one of the boys, a very thick book about chairs.

He sat close to me on the couch and I wanted time
to stop for a moment so we could go on forever

turning page after page of glossy color photographs
of all the different colors and types of chairs.

Christmas ended, and New Year's. The book dissolved,
all of it did, as though it had never happened.

A few months later, I dreamed that I was a doll,
walking on my little legs through the chair museum.

Next door was the table museum, and on the other side
of it was the spoon museum, and so on. You get the idea.

The chairs in my museum were very large,
and I felt so small as I walked between them.

I wasn't sure why I was there, or what I was supposed to be
learning, but I knew that I had to be there for a reason.

So all night, I walked around in my little stockings and
my little black felt slippers with the straps across the tops.

All night, I walked around and around the museum,
peeking up at chairs through my little glass eyes,

certain that all of the answers were right there in front of me
if only I knew where to look.

Approaching the Intersection of Princess and Bath

The first morning, I woke up feverish, shaking.
It was the thinnest filament of pain, drawn tight

over my left breast. I ran from tree to tree,
hewing to the shadows, my knife at my side.

The dogs followed, their paws as soundless
as my boots on the leaves and needles

of the forest floor. We emerged into daylight,
at the edge of the old limestone quarries,

looking for the blocks that were used to build
the towering cathedrals of an unknown city.

The tunnel from the crypt to the hospital was already
obstructed. Three years later, he flew to St. Petersburg.

For 100 rubles, a woman dressed as a Russian empress
offered to pose for photographs with tourists.

A man in the street was trying to sell cans of caviar
out of a gym bag. The man at the door had had the same one

when he arrived to pack the house, hours late, disheveled
and sweating whiskey. Still, I let him in because I needed

the help. We were picking the pinkest crabapples
and holding them out in our palms, waiting for horses.

On the last day in Minnesota, we loaded the remaining
boxes into the truck and drove north to Canada.

Crossing the Border

The guards stopped us at the border.
We were no longer American tourists
hoping to experience a day
of benign interaction or see
Niagara Falls from the Canadian side
and so they sequestered us
in the customs building while
they asked questions and studied
our passports and paperwork.

Everything we owned
was traveling separately,
would have to be claimed and identified
and imported later; this meeting
was just about us, our family,
our modest credentials
and aspirations.
It was the first time I had ever known myself
as an immigrant.

In the house we rented there,
one of the neighbors had never
traveled to the United States.
Was it safe, he wanted to know, to walk
on the sidewalks? It was a question
I didn't even understand
at first. I had never seen my country
through the transportive lens of American
movies. Absurd violence, everyone pointing

a gun. At school, one of my children
threatened another child.
The teacher called me in
for a meeting, sat me down
in front of her desk. *This might be*

*acceptable behavior
where you are from,*
she said, *but it won't be tolerated
here in Canada.*

One night, not long after,
a taxi driver was stabbed
and left to die on a sidewalk
just south of Princess Street.
The man who robbed him
abandoned the taxi but got away
with the cash and perhaps with
the crime. (Three years later, a jury
found the accused killer not guilty.)

When we entered the country,
my husband and I were each granted
a work permit good for three years.
We drove across the border into New York
and took the kids to the mall. It was the first
time we'd gone back. I missed Target
and Kinko's and Symphony bars. The most
pedestrian things you can imagine. But
we weren't used to being outsiders

and we forgot the work permits at home
and so when we tried to return
the Canadian guards stopped us
at the border. They made us pull the car
over to one side while they looked at
the American passports and the Ontario plates
and typed things into their computers
and we thought about our rented house
with the spiders in the basement

and the nautical-themed paintings
and the clothesline in the back yard
and the little kitchen where our eldest son
had accidentally burned the pancakes, and our cats
and our clothes and shoes and books
and the children's toys
and everything we'd left behind
while they decided whether or not
to let us back in.

Charley Horse

Just before he was supposed to leave Italy,
he woke in the night with a charley horse.

All the next day, he was in pain, limping.
After breakfast, he brought down his suitcase

and lingered in the lobby of the hotel,
talking to the man from Moldova

who'd drunk too much cognac the night before
and was nursing a hangover. They were still

talking when the car arrived to take him
to the airport; he said goodbye to the man

from Moldova and waved from the car window;
he was already at the airport when he realized

that he'd left his brown bag in the hotel lobby.
The laptop, all the notes for his next talk—

everything is a math problem now.
(If a driver travels at x kilometers per hour,

and the distance between the hotel and the airport
is y kilometers, how many minutes do you have

to get through security and limp all the way down
to the appropriate gate before ticketed passengers

must be on board the flight leaving for Germany?)
A very young woman with a stroller returns

to the service counter and elbows her way
in front of him, screaming at the desk clerks

in ragged Italian. She is wearing overalls, her blond
hair cut short, and the boy in the stroller

doesn't look up. The Italian women
with their sleek black hair and painted nails

are accustomed to this sort of thing;
they go on typing even as they snap back at her.

Later, on a sort of bus out to the tarmac,
the young woman will have to relinquish

the stroller and hold the little boy on her lap.
You can see: the fight has gone out of her.

They have all been herded onto this shuttle,
exhausted, drained, submissive as lambs.

The party is only half over, but the champagne
tastes flat and the hors d'oeuvres have gone cold.

Two weeks later, a shipping service will return
the brown bag to his home for 150 euros.

Someday he will hold his own sons on his lap.
Now, he stares out the window and waits.

Peripheral Vision

in the dark, a man stands waiting to cross the street
with a white plastic takeout bag in each hand

as I drive past on the sidewalk next to me a tall figure
wrapped in a white sheet, a face, something like a face

and a man speaks to me through our open car windows
as I pause at a red light, he's just making small talk

as if we are in a waiting room reading magazines
and he too is lonely, as all ghosts are lonely

Horseshoe Falls

The book on tape lasted almost exactly four hours:
just the right amount of time to get from Kingston
to Buffalo with one stop along the way.

I checked in to the hotel, a room too big
for one person, with a kitchenette and a miniature
living room and stairs leading up to the bedroom.

The reading was later that night, in an auditorium
nearby, and I sat numbly in front of the television
not knowing what else to do. I didn't remember how

to be alone. It was so rare then. A few days earlier,
I had been sitting in my car outside a doctor's office
after the exam was over, waiting for the pain to subside

so I could drive home. A woman pulled sideways
into the space in front of mine and when she tried to correct
herself accidentally backed into the front of my car.

She was an older woman, neatly dressed,
late for an appointment and on the verge of tears,
as I was, and if we had known each other

we could have hugged and offered consolation,
but we were strangers and so she apologized and I said
everything was fine, and we went our separate ways.

I would never know her if I saw her again, so
it may have been our only point of intersection
in this life. Or it may not have been. (Was it?)

In Buffalo I left the hotel room almost untouched
and drove to Niagara Falls the next morning.
I was planning to go home using a different route,

north and around through Hamilton and Mississauga.
I stood against a metal railing overlooking the falls
and looked from the United States into Canada

and felt a wave of homesickness, though I couldn't
have said for which place. At that time in my life,
I felt an almost equal sense of dislocation

no matter which side of the border I found myself on.
I didn't belong anywhere.
At the same time, it was like loving two good women:

I was torn between them
and yet lying next to either, I cried
and couldn't believe my luck.

Vancouver-Beijing

The day you left, you sent me a message,
a single line on your way to what I used to think
was the other side of the world:
About to board, Vancouver-Beijing.

I don't remember whether I answered.
For days, you kept up a chatty correspondence:
You got a traditional massage,
you reluctantly tried a bite of roasted durian.

It was near midnight there when you called
and told you me that you'd visited Tiananmen
Square. It was fifteen hours earlier
in California, the morning of the same day.

We hung up and you went to sleep.
It was already the next day in Beijing
when I saw the BBC News report
about the attack in Tiananmen Square.

After you left the site, a vehicle drove into
a crowd of tourists, then caught fire. Five people
had been killed, almost forty injured. Black smoke
flowed up from the burning wreckage.

The following June, eight people were sentenced
for their roles in planning the attack. Five received
prison sentences: five to twenty years, and for one, life.
The other three were sentenced to death.

Xinhua News Agency reported that they
had traveled to Beijing earlier that October
to deliver money to buy what was needed.
A jeep, for example. Gasoline, knives.

At some point, they must have gone
to sleep, tired after a long day's work.
It was fifteen hours earlier, then,
here in California. I was pouring milk

into a glass, scrambling eggs. The cat
rested his head for a moment against my leg.
You were climbing the ladder into the attic,
whistling, pulling down your suitcase.

Any Day Now

The test results are due back
any day now.

Life is like a mouse,
sniffing around me,

and I am a doll,
on the floor on my side,

lying where someone
has flung me.

At some point
the telephone will ring

and the wooden hinge
of my arm

will bend in its direction,
but I will let it go on ringing

for a moment
with that face at my neck

because I want to remember
at least once more

the scent of the lemon tree
in the back yard

and the view of the shoreline
on a windy day

and everything else
I've ever seen

in this world, which is so frightening
and wondrous

Milk (1983)

For the party
after his Bar Mitzvah,
his grandparents hired
a magician.

After the temple ceremony
and the dinner,
he was made to lie on his side
on a long table

in front of his family
and all of his friends
while the magician poured a pitcher of milk
into his ear.

There are so many
moments in life
when we want
to roll back time,

to pull the sword
out of a neck,
or watch milk spring back
into a pitcher.

When we wish
we had had the courage
to walk away
or say no

or stand up
for someone else.
Now he is
as brave as anyone.

But he was thirteen then,
and he did not know how
to do these things yet
so he lay down

and watched as the magician
pulled a rainbow
of brightly colored squares of silk
from a sleeve.

They told him
to be a good boy
and he was so new, still,
at being a man.

March 1, 2012

The cat has been missing for three days.
At five o'clock in the morning, the phone rings,
waking him out of a sound sleep,
and his first thought is that it's Christopher,
calling from wherever he has found himself,
and in his half-sleep, he is so puzzled by this—
the idea that Christopher has somehow
taught himself to dial the telephone.

It's not him, of course—it's an old friend,
still back on the east coast, who has forgotten
about the time difference and is already
at the office, his day already in progress.

The two men end the phone call, and back
on the west coast, though it is still so early,
he pads down to the kitchen in his socks
and turns on the coffee pot, listening
to its familiar, comforting sounds as he peers
out into the darkness of the backyard,
trying to catch a glimpse of Christopher.

This is the second cat who's gone missing
in his life, so even though he's put out food
and water and hung up posters in the neighborhood,
he knows that it's hopeless. This is the cat
that his son named when he was six, the one
with paws that are gray on top and black underneath.

Standing at the back window, he has no way of knowing
that Christopher will return within two weeks, hoarse
as if from screaming. He has no way of knowing
anything, it seems, except the blank feeling

of being awake too early and the scent of the coffee
brewing on the countertop and his own reflection
in the dark window and the unexpected possibilities
of a telephone call that could be coming from anywhere.

The Most Fragile Part of the Human Body

In Pennsylvania, the boys slept
on matching twin beds.

They were both six,
my son and my nephew.

Each night, they flitted
from one subject to the next.

My son said, *I will play
with cars every day,*

on and on, until the day I die,
and my nephew answered,

without hesitation, *Our bodies
may die, but our spirits live on.*

From the next room, I heard
their segue to another topic.

Now we are back home,
and your father has been

in the hospital again.
This time, the doctors removed

a clutch of new tumors, and also
a portion of his shoulder blade.

I thought I read, one time,
that the neck

is the most fragile part
of the human body.

But I can't remember
where I saw this, or when,

and searching for the truth
reveals nothing certain.

When you describe the pain
of the missing bone, it seems

that truly, the most fragile part is always
the one that has been most damaged.

The tumors are spreading
rapidly, extravagantly.

Your heart beats too fast
every time the phone rings.

At night, sometimes, I look out
at the streetlamps.

Each one casts
a small circle of light,

but strung together, they form
a path to follow.

At night, sometimes, it seems
that we are all six-year-old boys,

lying on our matching twin beds
in a dark room,

keeping each other company
as best we can,

while we are suspended here
indefinitely,

in the long night-stretch
between life and death.

Take a Seat

I wake up halfway to the island.
We flew in earlier from Vienna,
where there was an art installation
in a secured area of the airport:
two rows of waiting-room chairs
had been mounted to the wall.
The title of the piece was "take a seat."

We're an hour outside of Zagreb,
with an hour left to go. I'm
in the back seat, still half-asleep, still
lying against my suitcase. The engine
of the car is in the trunk and there is
only enough room left over for yours.
Outside is a thick blanket of fog.

We're sailing through it faster
than I've ever gone in my life,
passing other cars, or what I can see
of them, taking no notice of signals
or stop signs, the radio still playing
and over it the sound of his wife, begging him
to slow down on the hairpin turns,

but in my hazy state I don't mind
that we could die tonight halfway
between Zagreb and the Island of Krk.
It is warm in the car—pleasant, even.
We haven't yet had our tea and cake,
haven't knelt in the courtyard of the church
and lit candles for the dead.

But these sequences won't go unclaimed.
They will merely slip back into the ether
for someone else, who tomorrow
will wake up in a stranger's bed
with nails painted the color of new pennies
and breakfast already waiting
on a balcony overlooking the sea.

Lucky Stars

I saw you again last night
in my rearview mirror

when I stopped at a red light.
You were driving the car

behind me, hands on ten
and two, your hair dark

again and a little too long,
facing away, keeping time

with a song on the radio.
Everything around us

was discolored
from the sodium vapor lighting

that once turned a white car red,
the witness so adamant

that the detectives assigned to the case
spent years searching for the wrong man.

In Russian, a misfit
is not a black sheep

but a white crow,
white,

white as snow, white as birch trees,
white as the faux fur

she bent over
night after night

at her sewing table,
cutting and pinning the ears

of one of the many costumes
that turned him into an animal.

White as the reams of paper
in their bankers boxes,

as the bleached skull
they found in the desert.

White as the stars, though, too,
overhead as the traffic light turns green

and this embodiment of you
turns in a different direction

and I release myself from the dazzling cage
of city streets

and go forward
until nothing is visible but the night sky

and below it the black asphalt
unwinding endlessly in front of me.

There's Nothing

There's nothing I can tell you
that you don't already know.

The color of the irises
in the flower bed outside the window,

the spring of the dog's paws
against the lawn.

You kissed my throat,
the insides of my knees.

Sunlight slanted
through the room.

I can close my eyes now
and feel my back against the wooden floor.

On the Way Back to the Museum

It was the first time in San Francisco,
the time I saw a junkie step off the curb
in front of an oncoming car.

I was in a hurry, too; you were waiting
for me (or I thought you were)
and I didn't want to be late.

When I arrived, though, you were still
inside, behind the metal detector
and a wall of security guards with guns.

I stayed outside in the courtyard,
sitting on the stone steps of the church,
and when you finally emerged I was

on the phone with my daughter's
French teacher, who had dialed my
cell number and wanted to talk about cheating

while I sat so many miles away, on the stone steps
of a church in San Francisco, waiting for you.
The noise of the traffic was enormous,

drowning out the teacher's accented English
and your approaching footsteps
and the sharp brake of the taxi driver

on his way down the hill
(the scene still replaying in my mind)
as the junkie, at the last second,

broke out of his dream state
with my hand on the back of his sleeve
and stepped back onto the curb.

Dinner with Mohamoud

He tells a story about arriving in America
during wintertime. This was a foreign
climate, and winter had been described

in great detail. He was prepared
for cold, for snow, for icicles
hanging from every branch and rooftop.

In his suitcase, he had a warm coat
and gloves.

The airplane stopped on the way to Minnesota,
landing briefly in San Diego, and he pressed
his face against the small oval of window

for his first glimpse of America. Outside,
on the tarmac below, people moved about
in shorts and short-sleeved shirts,

their arms and legs bare, their pale skin
impervious to what he could only imagine
were freezing temperatures.

Now, in the restaurant, his eyes are dark
with fatigue. His sons are in a refugee camp
in Kenya, his wife dead. But tonight

they are close by, and it is all right to go on
laughing faintly about the nuances of weather,
unaware that we are another year away

from the airport where he will again see his boys,
almost men, their backs unbowed despite the weight
of all these shifts in the atmosphere.

The Night He Broke His Collarbone

The diaper commercials never show
all the waiting:

the outer room at the dentist or
the living room when he's out late or

at his bedside, in the emergency room,
waiting to take the X-rays or hear the results.

Or now, standing outside in the driveway
in the dark, waiting for the ambulance.

My son is sitting in the front
passenger seat of my car,

trying not to move too much
or cry or throw up, and

I stand in the wedge of light
from the car's open door.

Earlier tonight, when the sun was still low,
he hit a bump on the BMX track

and slammed into the ground
shoulder-first. He is not quite thirteen.

His friend had to borrow a cell phone
to call his father and ask him to drive over

and pick them up in his SUV.
At the time, it didn't seem so serious.

The neighbors have come outside,
one already in her nightdress and robe,

wringing her hands. There is nothing left
to say. Mostly, it is quiet. Other cars drive past,

and at the end of the street, a city bus stops
to collect its passengers before grinding away again.

One night, on a school trip, there was an accident—
but it was twenty years ago and all I remember now

is filing off a bus in the dark, and seeing
a teenage boy laid out on his back

in a parking lot, in some unfamiliar state—
in another lifetime, it seems now.

But it is all called back by the faint sound of the siren
rising from the bottom of the hill,

eliciting a familiar sense of relief. The ambulance
pulls to a stop in front of us, and the back doors are opened

to reveal its inner workings: the raised white cot,
the long gray bench, a series of cupboards, and then

the confident, efficient machine of the paramedics
emerging with their clipboards and backboard

and gloves and stethoscope,
and the pair of silver scissors they'll use

to cut his shirt off his body, deftly,
like magicians performing a deceptively complex trick,

and in that moment I almost expect to see rising smoke
and a flurry of milk-white doves

as they set aside the glittering mirror of the scissors
and whisk back the colored cloth.

Blue

The eyes, the dress, the pumps,
the blue and white gingham curtains
at the kitchen window—

The car, the seats, the steering wheel,
the wide expanse of sky
beyond the windshield—

In front of me, the dark tapers
of the trees, arranged in a row
in front of the blue mountains,

in front of the blue sky,
and funneling out from one point
the black outlines of birds—

The car is an extension
of my hands, my arms,
my entire body, which is

standing up, arms raised
overhead, as the birds fly through
my outstretched fingers—

And I find that
we are always falling backwards
into the pool,

trusting that the water
will be there
to receive us.

Time Zones

Irritable, stricken with jet lag,
we spent a long night in Paris
arguing over a grievance
so petty I could scarcely remember it
the following day.

It was our first vacation alone
since the birth of our first child,
it was my first time in Europe,
and it had taken so much to get
to that moment in the hotel room—

but then nothing was as it should
have been. All my years of French
seemed as useless there as they had
in Montreal, where we sat on the floor
of the airport waiting to see

if the plane would even take off.
It was the spring of 2010, when a cloud
of volcanic ash from Iceland
grounded flights across Europe—
an otherworldly scene

that unfolded on television as we spent
hours in the airport, surrounded by families
stranded on vacation in Canada
and unable to get home. We'd taken
the train from Kingston to Montreal

not knowing whether it would be possible
to continue until the woman from the airline
said, "Let's go to Paris," and everyone cheered
and got in a line behind her and walked toward
the plane in that celebratory mood

and so it was a minor miracle that we had
gotten to Europe at all, under the circumstances,
and we were squandering it by staying up late
in a hotel room with flowers on the table
and a balcony overlooking a Parisian courtyard

and wishing that this agony would end.
We had tickets to London for the next day
and rather than give them up we rose early
and arrived exhausted and still a little angry
and couldn't agree on anything to do

so we climbed the stairs to the top of a red
double decker tour bus and drove around
the city of London as a guide pointed out
Westminster Abbey and Big Ben. I fell
asleep and didn't wake up until the tour

was over and I'd missed everything,
but you put your arm around me and we stayed
on the bus and drove around the city a second time
because that's what this is, sometimes—
we keep waking up and waking up

and starting over
again.

Mid-Week

All night you've been sailing toward the bed,
that merciful shore in the distance
that seems to grow farther away
with every passing moment
because no matter where you walk
the dog's dish is empty
or the sink is full,
and now one of the children is sitting up in bed
calling out for a cup of water
and another long squeeze, trying
with those little arms to hold you here
forever. And even though the dark, elusive curtain
of sleep is shimmering all around you,
you don't loosen his arms and leave the room
because you don't know how long you have
before this moment becomes the mirage
that is always hovering
just beyond your reach.

When the Sun Comes Out After Three Days of Rain

My skin is plastered
with wet leaves
and flower petals

I'm still lying
on my back
on the sidewalk

but the wind
is in abeyance
at last

the restless edges
of my dress
have stopped moving

I've been lying here
on my back
for so long

I can barely remember
how to stand
or walk away

but I can see that the sky
is no longer a pale,
sickly gray ocean

the trees have lost
their leaves but the sky
is such a glorious blue

I Wrapped My Dishes in Newsprint

Years on, the sight of a moving van
began to incite a certain feeling in me,

hard to describe—equal parts,
perhaps, fear and exhilaration—

and I answered the phone, too,
with some dizzying combination

of anxiety and anticipation and dread
as I'd been conditioned over time to do.

We never knew who might be
on the other end of the line.

I was sometimes frightened, I admit—
bending my head and asking for guidance,

but the only direction in this world
is forward.

We accepted the deal.
We signed the contract.

There was no way to know
what the future held.

So I wrapped my dishes in newsprint
and pulled the curtains closed.

We drove away, we drove away.
I didn't know what to believe in

but the headlights
in front of us,

the sound of the engine
moving us through the night,

a new key waiting somewhere
on the other side.

In Transit

When we left Canada,
when we drove over the border
for the last time as
landed immigrants
and went back to being
ourselves, we went straight to
your aunt and uncle's house in Detroit,
the one they'd owned at that time
for forty-seven years,
and were able to say goodbye
to him—not knowing then
that it was goodbye—
before we flew to San Francisco.
Under my seat, undermedicated,
the cat cried in her carrier.
We'd signed over our cars
and almost everything we owned
and here we were again,
in limbo, in transition, in transit.
The family of red-necked grebes
floating on the surface of the lake
crack open their wings,
about to go up into the air
or down into the water,
but lingering, at least briefly,
before moving on
from this world
to the one that follows.

Imperial Butterfly House, Vienna

It is humid inside the Schmetterlinghaus,
everyone sweating in their coats and gloves,
while outside in the gardens it is 5 degrees Celsius
and the statues outside the Hofburg Royal Palace
are cold and imperious, looking down on all
of the tourists with their cameras and maps
while the Austrians wake up in the morning
and eat drink go to work read books have sex
have arguments look out the window go for a walk
the same way we would if we were at home
wherever we are from, but we are not there,
and so we have to unfold our maps and look
at our lists of places we have been and places
we have yet to go because we are always
searching for a small glass enclosure
filled with tropical plants and butterflies
in the middle of some metaphorical winter.

The First Day You Were in the Psychiatric Hospital

We visited twice, once in the afternoon
and once in the evening.

The second time, he took a miniature carton
of Häagen-Dazs ice cream (mint chocolate

chip, your favorite) and two plastic spoons.
I took a pair of brightly colored socks

with suns and moons and blue and purple cats
and a shower of sparkling golden stars.

You had lost so much weight that your skin,
that day, was almost translucent.

I can still remember how small and fragile
your fingers looked as he handed you a spoon.

But before we were allowed to go upstairs
to see you, we had to stop again at the security desk.

Your name was written in pen on a line in their book.
Already, you had been given a number.

I removed the keys and coins from my pockets,
prepared this time for the sudden intimacy

of the wand, brushing my outstretched arms
and the lengths of the backs of my legs.

Crossing from One Continent to the Next

*Had I known how much time would pass before we'd see each other again,
I would have said a different goodbye.*
—Karen Thompson Walker, *The Age of Miracles*

There is no way to know how many hours you have
spent awake, pacing up and down the hallway
outside my bedroom door. All night, perhaps,
the thoughts scattered and gathered again,
circling in the darkness like small, restless birds.

I find you at dawn. I have been afraid for so long
that it is almost a relief to come to the end, to know
that we have finally reached the distinct separation
between water and land. You are a stranger now,
and we no longer speak a common language,

but this seems somehow unsurprising, inevitable.
Without knowing it, all these months, we've been
preparing to cross the ocean at night, and the fear
of leaving is only less than the fear of staying still.
By the time the ambulance arrives at the office,

it is close to dinnertime, and you've worn yourself
hoarse. All day, I have seen occasional flickers of you,
of the person I remember, as one might catch
a glimpse of a stone or shell beneath a shallow wave
before the ocean water carries it out of sight again.

There are two paramedics, and they help you onto a gurney
and tie you down with straps. You are shaking,
despite your jacket, and they cover you with a heavy
blue blanket. We will not be allowed to go inside
the hospital tonight, so we have to let them lift you

into the back of the ambulance and close the doors.
The grass grows high under my feet, seasons change,
this world becomes another world. I grow old and die
a thousand deaths and still I go on standing there,
watching that ambulance take you away from me.

Visiting Hours

It was such a cold summer.
The wind fought against the car
as we drove almost sixty miles
to get to you. Every day
we refined our route,
choosing the best time
to leave the house,
the least congested roads.
It is difficult to describe
the feeling I had driving there—
the specific combination
of anticipation and dread—
or the one that followed
on the return trip: faint hope one day,
despair the next. We had no map
to follow, no way of knowing
what landmarks to look for.
Every day we passed the billboard
promoting an exhibit of sea jellies
at the aquarium, big signs directing
us toward the airport. Planes
ascended in front of us
but we never tried to escape.
It was a strange life, sailing past
the inflated pink bell of the jelly,
the lingering tentacles, always
floating overhead. Every night
we had to put on our coats
before we left the building;
even the short walk to the car
was bitterly cold in that wind.

The Blue Room

The nurse had called that morning
to talk about release, and when I arrived
that evening, you and I sailed toward each other
from opposite ends of a long hallway,
both of us buoyant. You had changed
out of the scrubs and into your clothes
we had brought from home, and you looked
like yourself again. When I pulled you close,
I remember the clean scent of your skin and hair.

The nurse unlocked a room I had never seen
before, a small windowless cube
containing only a table and two chairs.
The pale blue walls lacked even the most basic
ornamentation; unlike the other rooms,
there were no books or signs or games,
no props to hang a casual conversation on.
But you were smiling. I had brought you,
wrapped in a napkin, a sweet summer peach
that I had cut in the car before walking inside.

I put you under hypnosis, you said. Bring
another peach when you come tomorrow,
and you will be released. I was not under
hypnosis, I did not think, but the nurse
had left and closed the door behind her.
I looked for the clock, to see how long we had
until she came back, but there were no clocks
in this blue room. It doesn't matter,
you said. There are no clocks at all in this place.

But there are, I said. I've seen them,
in the library and behind the nurses' station.
Yes, you said patiently. They are there,
but they don't work. There is no time here.
Again and again we had gone over the dates,
and the days; what had happened before
you went into the hospital, and since.
Often you compressed these events
into a single day or two, convinced that
you'd been at work earlier that morning.

Alone with you in the blue room, these distortions
of reality began to seem possible. I leaned forward,
deflated. I knew that the meeting in the morning
would be postponed, the release date
pushed forward. Tonight things will go badly,
you say. There will be a number of phone calls.
Am I still sitting there in the blue room when
the telephone rings at four o'clock in the morning
and I hear your voice, telling me that you love me?

Driving Alone at Night on an Unfamiliar Highway (November)

Things are moving too fast:
an endless snake of white lights
flying toward me in the dark.
If I could just close my eyes
and put my head down for a minute
things might be all right,
but there's no way to stop.
The lights are too bright,
and I haven't reached my destination,
and there are no exits.
It's an unfamiliar car, an unfamiliar road—
no sense of where it's going
or when—
the car rental papers
(like hospital discharge papers)
in the bag on the seat beside me.

Time Loops Back on Itself

> *This was maybe yesterday or maybe last year. It was in the house on the coast or it was in my childhood home or it was somewhere I can't remember now. I pick through the rubble of my brain. My brain is an archaeological site.*
>
> —Marya Hornbacher, *Madness*

Three or four months may not seem like much
in the span of a lifetime, especially when viewed
at a comfortable distance, but the beds have been
stripped of their linens, the baby will never be fed;
every inch of skin is chafed, and the bones remain unset.
My mind is a catalogue now of all the different
medications, their dosages and side effects, the dates
we began or increased or began to cross-taper,
and after a while I can scarcely remember a life
before this one; what we want to reclaim has been absent
so long that it is almost impossible to remember.
At group, one of the mothers says that she has stopped
going out with friends. You can only talk about it
with other people for so long, I know. It is exhausting
but inescapable. I remember a young guard at the hospital,
once, asking me where we were headed after a visit, maybe
on our way to a movie. Was there a time, then,
when I thought of something other than the diagnosis,
or the fear that it would wind through the family like
the fine hooked tendrils of some deceptive, virulent plant?
You are an adult, a teenager, a child. The medication
has finally brought you down, and now, in the morning,
I have to lift you out of bed. This is Kafka, after
the metamorphosis, but we're alone with the insect's
untenanted exoskeleton, waiting. Time loops back on itself.
I prop you up on pillows, I feed you breakfast.
Months pass. Each fragment its own sunless autumn, one o'clock.

Paris

Every day now we wake
in an unexpected hotel room.

Will this be the afternoon
in Paris, with birds singing

in the courtyard
below our window?

Or, more likely, will we find ourselves
somewhere else entirely. Most days,

the room is either too hot
or too cold, or an unsettling

combination of both;
the sun angles in through

ill-fitting curtains, or
we've been woken in the night

by loud, frightening noises:
fists pounding on a door, sirens.

It's too late or too early,
and we've traveled too long;

it's the night I was pregnant
and we were moving cross-country,

or the morning after any sleepless,
swollen night. The headache

won't go away, or we're back in
Toronto, in the hotel with the

wedding reception down the hall
from our room, the blaring music

and the fight that went on so long
that someone called the police.

There are so many bad days.
Every morning, though, I wake up

hoping for just one more golden afternoon
(so lovely and heartbreaking),

for sunlight in the courtyard
and birdsong.

Cutting

The night you were born, there was an emergency
and the surgery had to be postponed by two hours.

All that time, I was lying in a hospital bed
imagining the doctor pressing a knife

or the blade of a box cutter
against the soft flesh of my stomach.

At that time, I didn't know about all the layers—
the excavation required—the interior strata

between my skin and yours.
There were so many things

I couldn't envision at that time,
such as the possibility that you might,

one day, take the kitchen knives
that I use to chop onions

and test the various blades
against the thin blue veins of your wrists.

But go back to the hospital room.
To me, lying in my gown, looking up

at a television mounted on the wall
in front of me, projecting a small mirror image

of me in the bed in my hospital gown
and your father standing next to me.

Both of us unable to imagine
what would happen next.

Problems (#1)

You get home from school
at 3 p.m.

The bell at your brother's
elementary school rings at 3 p.m.

His school is 10 minutes away
from our house.

What time will it be
if I get home too late?

Problems (#2)

How could I go on living
without you?

Calling 911

The first two nights he was in Amherst,
I lay in that big bed alone and had nightmares.

I was walking with you along a dark street.
A man was performing tricks with oversized knives,

throwing them up in the air, the silver gleaming
in the moonlight, and catching them in his hands

and teeth. Throwing, catching, throwing.
But he made an error, timed something wrong,

and accidentally cut the skin of his face into pieces.
Blood bubbled up from these hastily ripped seams

in a slow, surprised way at first, then at a steady pace;
the man sank to his knees, fingers slick with blood.

Over and over, I tried to dial 911,
but my hands were shaking so badly

that I kept making mistakes. All night, I went on trying,
fumbling doggedly with the numbers on that little phone,

while a man lay on the ground, bleeding to death
because I couldn't make the call for help,

and you stood at my side, watching, motionless,
waiting for me to set things right.

Spring Arrives Late

Suddenly, the rosebushes are all in bloom,
covered in enormous, extravagant roses,
and it is as if I have never seen light before,
the way it illuminates each leaf and petal.
They look almost unnatural, otherworldly.

The miniature green peaches on the peach tree
are doubling and redoubling in size and number;
I stop counting when I get to one hundred.

On Sunday afternoon, we decide to walk
in a new direction, on an endless hiking path.
I am exhausted by the time we reach the top
of the dusty hill and look down, where I expect
the grim path to continue indefinitely in front of us.

Instead, there is a wide reservoir,
glistening in the sunlight, surrounded by a grove
of trees, and on a faraway path along the shore,
a father and his daughter riding their bikes. Farther still,
a little boy, holding the string of a distant red kite.

I've waited so long for you. Months, then years. It's necessary
to study you, to take note of each new line and gesture,
everything that still makes you laugh. But now, here, I find

that the sky is so blue and the water so bright. I don't want
to leave anything unsaid, but we are both rendered speechless
by the sight of this body of water, by the incomprehensible extent
of beauty in the world. Looking out at it, I can believe,
for a moment, that this time, you might be able to stay.

Almost a Year After His Suicide

After a glass of wine, it no longer seems possible
that he's dead. You weren't close, toward the end
of his life, and it's been months since he has floated
into your thoughts, unbidden, out of the blue.

Now, sitting on the back porch,
you can remember every line
of his last letter. He had sounded at peace
then, just a few short weeks before.

The wisteria is in bloom, with its thick,
fragrant bunches of lavender flowers,
and the lemon tree is heavy with fruit.
At sunset, the dead seem close by,

present, lingering in your peripheral vision.
And for a moment, in the golden light,
this has to be heaven, because how could anyone
truly be dead, here amidst so much beauty?

Encyclopedia Britannica

Time was a languorous thing once—
a long summer day spent lying on your
side eating a chocolate chip ice cream cone
and pushing the porch swing idly with one foot,
listening to the hum of cicadas in the trees
or the similarly dreamlike sound of ocean water
lapping at the shore. We used to spend
hours lying on the couch in the basement
taking off each other's clothes, the scent
of his neck the sweetest thing I could imagine,
and this is sometimes what I thought of
at night as I was falling asleep under the open window
and this is also what I am thinking of
when one of the kids pulls a cellphone
out of a pocket and asks me what in the world
we ever did without them.

More Than 1,000 Dead Birds Fall from the Sky in Arkansas

It sounds like a scene
from a horror movie.

The sounds of
screaming, running—

of small feathered bodies
hitting parked cars

and the neighbors'
newly shingled roof.

There should be smoke
rising in the air,

a burnt smell, the persistent
sound of sirens.

No one knows why this happened
though there are theories.

It seems like a warning, a sign,
some kind of foreshadowing.

But it is difficult to piece
these things together,

even for the scientists,
and the fear and helplessness

can't change anything.
Sometimes it is necessary

for each person to give and then
have faith in people and nature

because although the birds
are real, this is, too:

Outside it is January,
but here inside the house

the cat is warm and drowsy
in the sun, and there is

a fresh cup of coffee
and the crisp sound

of the newspaper pages
as they turn toward each other

and so many other small signs
and portents.

A Common Language

In the Emergency Room, that first time,
the man at the front desk read questions
off a computer screen. The woman
whose back had seized up as she tried to lift
a laundry basket, whose husband held
her arm as she took each hunched, painful
step, or the boy whose mother had wrapped
cotton towels around his bleeding wrist.
When it was our turn, when you said
anorexia, the first question he asked was,
"Have you eaten anything today?"
It was 10:30 at night. In the waiting room,
for a brief time, every group of people
spoke a different language. We were
our own island, sitting there, but at last
we had found a place where we no longer
had to smile and make small talk
and pretend that everything was all right.
Everyone in the room had also been,
in some way, shattered. Later, when you
were released from the psychiatric hospital,
one line on your papers said "Anorexia,
in remission," and I was naïve enough
to believe that it would last, that the bear
would never come out of hibernation.
Or, at times, that it had never existed at all.

But that winter, as you gathered your strength,
I could hear it, stirring under the snow.

Damage

One has to question the logic of a swing set
embedded in a slab of asphalt
on the playground of an elementary school.

Those coltish legs slanted at an angle,
the dark smile of each seat hanging from chains,
but it was the 1970s all plaid slacks

and big collars and we didn't think about safety
then, in those years before AIDS and baby
car seats. It was still cool to smoke and sunbathe,

and I never had to wear a bike helmet
or travel en masse because the weirdo
in the white van who stopped me

on my way to school and asked if I'd seen his dog
and would I get in and help him look for it
was an anomaly, and we didn't lock

our front door or worry about picking up
a woman stranded by the side of the road
with her car because nobody had a cell phone

and looking back my god it's a wonder we
didn't all die; it's a wonder anyone survived
with all the lead paint and raw cookie dough.

So I never thought twice about the bed of asphalt
waiting for Jason Jackson's warm head
as he stood on the swing and pushed as hard

as he could with his legs. That swing set
is gone now, and the spinning death trap
we used to fall off of and even the teeter-totters,

with their pale splintered wood, but they were still
there then. And Jason didn't die, just cracked
his head open on the asphalt and had to go

to the hospital in an ambulance and get stitches.
Every day from then on his father went to work
a little later because he walked him to school

carrying Jason's little sister on his shoulders
in a fog of cigarette smoke, and all three of them smiling
as if it were the victory march.

American Housewife

Go back to 1952
or '54—
your choice—
and plug your state-of-the-art
vacuum cleaner
into the wall.
There are the carpets
and the rugs
and the special attachment
for the drapes
and the most powerful nozzle
guaranteed to take the calendar
right off the wall
and your shopping lists
for the next day
and the day after that
and the carrots and potatoes
on the kitchen counter
waiting to be peeled
and put in the oven
for dinner
and the homework
on the table
and the children
in their beds
where you've left them
since this morning
like paper dolls
because you're not in the mood
to play with them today
and your husband—
your husband—
you can catch him
at the door

when he comes home
from work
looking for a dry
martini and a hot
steak and a patient woman
to lie underneath
him so that he
can finish his day off
right.

Suburban Dreams

The grass is cut so perfectly
that you could measure it with a ruler

and your rose bushes are the envy
of the neighborhood

Sally has practiced her scales
until she could play them in her sleep

and Mrs. Woodard wants her
to play in a special recital next month

(because with the last teacher
you could play for fun

but this one is dry and humorless
with a list of strict instructions

and #1 is never let my cat out
when you come for your lesson

though the cat is nowhere near the door
and you're not a dummy

but she thinks that you are
and addresses you as such)

but it's all right because the meatloaf
will turn out perfectly and the potatoes

roasted in their jackets with coarse
Kosher salt and thick pats of butter

and in summer you take the kids for a week
at the lake where he grills burgers

and you split open a watermelon so sweet and red
it makes your eyes burn

and you go to church on Sunday
and cheer on the team

and take a Jell-O salad
to the potluck

the one you like with the cherries
and whipped cream and marshmallows

and it's the best Jell-O salad
anyone's had and they ask for your recipe

and maybe that night Bill
from two doors away

will think of you
while he's going down on his wife

because it's too early for key parties yet—
you've still got a decade or two—

so in the meantime you win
ribbons for your needlepoint

and iron the bedsheets so smooth
that you sleep like an angel

and wake with your hair
perfectly coiffed

and your teeth already brushed
and the coffee percolating

and the dishes washed
and breakfast on the table

and the children's clothes
starched on their hangers

the dog's nails clicking on the linoleum
and the sun glinting in the window

through a freshly washed pane
onto your fine pink fingernails

and your glossy, glossy hair
and everything that sparkles and shines.

A Cupboard Full of Keys

Where is the one
that ends the charade?

The war is over
and for a while it was enough

to coast along
on good feelings.

There was a ring on every finger
and a baby on every hip,

but now that it's been a few years
you find that you bring out

whole sides of each other
that you wish you could put away again

and you start to notice
the young mechanic

who services your car
or the milkman or the man

who brings a letter to your door.
You want him

and maybe he wants you,
but it's too late—

you've already made
your choices

and aren't you lucky, really?
The world is full of men

with their legs blown off
lying in hospital beds,

the world is full of pain and death
and destruction and here you are

complaining because
the baby is crying

or the darkness won't lift.

The world is full of doors
and all you have to do

is turn on the gas,
young mother,

or will you too be trapped
by love, or necessity,

because there are so many different ways
to suffer.

Open the Door

Put the roast in the oven
Ice the cake
Pull the plates from the breakfront

Dress the salad in a cut crystal bowl
Lay silver and glass on the tablecloth
Put a record on

Call the children in from the yard
Give the dog a treat
Give your husband a kiss

Lie down at night
In the world that you built
With your own two hands

And thank God
That you made it through
Another day

Wednesday Afternoon

on the last day of my cat's life
we sat in the waiting room at the vet
with an old, sick dog who kept
resting his head against my knee

the TV on the wall was turned down
too low for me to hear
but on the news an 18-year-old girl had been
stabbed to death outside a BART train

a video showed people lined up
along the walls of a station
lying on the ground in sleeping bags
and on the train a used needle
was sticking out of a seat cushion

at a stoplight on the way here
a boy sat in the passenger seat
of his dad's truck
with his hands over his face
and a hospital band on one wrist

for some reason I thought of the girl
who meant to make a light cut
but sliced her arm so deeply
that she had to have surgery

on the radio they're saying
Demi Lovato OD'd on heroin
and the college student in Iowa
who went out for a run is still missing

in front of me a young woman
with long hair dyed purple
and pulled back in a ponytail
crosses the street without looking up

and it's obviously hopeless but still
everyone goes on trying

In the Valley

Backdrop. It was a place
where you could buy a house
for 80K. That was a little
then, even less now. We used to
go to Vannie Tilden's
& look in the bakery cases,
& I was allowed to get anything
I wanted, though in the end it was always
a cream horn on a tiny white plate
& a cup of coffee for you.

Paperbacks were a dollar
& change at the bookstore
& you let me get a stack at a time,
& we drove down to the beach
& stayed in a motel with a big,
old-fashioned key, & when I think back
to that time I wish I could go back
& crawl up onto the big four-poster bed
next to you the way I did every morning
while you were still asleep.

I was too young then to be afraid
that you might not wake up—
or (worse?) might not want to wake up.
He was already dead then
but you were still alive,
so we drove down to Mexico
& went to a restaurant in Matamoros
where a man lit a cigarette
at his table between
our booth & the front door.

We sat in the dark
& watched
as the smoke drifted slowly
toward the ceiling.

Texas

Where are you sitting when *Wheel of Fortune* comes on?
When Vanna White crosses the stage in her floor-length gown
and touches her fingers to the bright green tiles
until they become something else?

It could be almost any day of the week. Pat Sajak with his suit
and friendly banter, bending at the waist to spin the wheel.
I used to sit on the green shag carpet in the living room
while you cooked dinner just down the hall.

He died in that kitchen, and now I think how difficult
it must have been to walk in there every day, but what can you do
in this life? I used to sleep in my uncle's old room with
the bookshelves full of books and the enormous mahogany desk.

The grass in the yard was thick and scratched my ankles
and in summer it was too hot even under the palm trees
but back inside Tom Selleck is young again, gliding across
the screen, and you are in the kitchen, and I wish it would never
    end.

We Argue About the Aesthetics of Garbage

The green couch, its pale arm peeled back
to reveal cardboard and staples, leaks
clumps of stuffing across the grass.

We've carried it all the way up from the basement,
lifted it over the railing, pinched our fingers
shimmying it through the doorway.

This is the first furniture we ever bought together,
now marred by claw marks and baby vomit,
the threadbare pillow covers peeled off and washed

a hundred times. All night, the couch will sit outside
in the dark, supporting an old stroller's spongy handle,
pieced back together with strips of clear duct tape.

At first, we are laughing as I adjust the couch,
placing it perpendicular to the lip of black asphalt,
and neatly stack the discarded paper boxes

on the grass next to the trash can. "Leave it be,"
you finally say, and when I refuse, you go inside
without me. I move each item until it is just

where it should be, and then I lie down
on the green couch and watch cars drive by
this precise and orderly arrangement.

Instincts

> *Squirrels don't have to learn how to hide the nuts they gather. . . .*
> *Even squirrels raised in cages have these instincts. The first time they're given nuts, they try to dig holes in the bottom of their cages. Then they shove the nuts into the imaginary holes and work their paws around as if they're covering the nuts with soil or leaves.*
> —Diane Swanson, *Welcome to the World of Squirrels*

Tree squirrels are helpless
at birth, just hairless pink bodies
the size of a woman's thumb,
eyes and ears sealed shut,
all huddled together for warmth
on this quilt of leaves and moss.

Yet somehow they know how
to find their mother, to nurse;
they grow a faint layer of fur
and blink in the sunlight.
Within a few months, they can leave
the nest behind: they've learned

how to groom themselves
and search for solid food
and later have babies of their own.
They wear matching gold bands
and move to the suburbs,
buy a big house with a

finished basement and a 30-year
fixed-rate mortgage and a membership
to the community pool,
but sometimes their grown daughter
will still sneak downstairs
in the middle of the night

while her babies are snug in their
matching cribs and flannel sleepers with feet,
their bellies full of formula, her head full of
grocery lists and news stories and bank statements,
and try to dig her way out of the cold
and the concrete to reach the forest floor.

Refrain

Every evening now I serve you butter chicken
all cream and cardamom on a bed of jasmine rice
with a bottle of Black Sheep Ale imported from England
and later we make love with the lights turned off
for the first time in almost a month
and I don't know what any of this means
the night that clicks down like a worn but well-loved record
from a happier time even as we sit at the table
with cloth napkins in our laps and warm food
in our mouths that don't remember how to speak
or how to say goodbye.

Looking for What Is Lost

The neighbor girls bring over
a plastic trash can full of bunnies.

Not favorite rabbits from childhood,
wilted from too much love and saliva,

but live baby bunnies, eight of them,
huddled close together in the bottom

of a trash can. The two sisters turn
the container on its side and let the bunnies

loose on my lawn, where they eat grass
and twitch their noses, like bunnies

in cartoons. One of the girls tells me
that a few days earlier, one of the babies

disappeared in the woods behind their house.
The sisters chased him for hours,

but they were not able to find him. The girl
telling the story lifts her pants at the knee

and points to her bare shin. *Poison ivy,*
she says. *We didn't know it was there.*

The other sister shrugs. She, too, is wearing
pants in 90-degree weather. Later that night,

I sit on my back porch where it's breezy
and cool. I drink beer and look at the stars,

thinking of the smallest baby bunny, who fell
asleep in the palm of my hand.

Now I stare into the woods hopefully,
half-expecting to see two eyes,

the twitch of a baby bunny nose. He'd appear,
the lost one, first of a long, slow, shy procession

of lost creatures, on their way home at last. There'd
be stuffed animals dropped from strollers, dogs

and cats who slipped out sliding-glass doors,
the boy who vanished last November.

They've been huddled together, I imagine, waiting
for someone to come and lead them all back.

I am hoping to see a flash of white bunny tail,
moonlight falling on gray fur and blond hair.

But the woods are dark and impassive, and no
matter how hard I look, there are no signs of life.

A White Boat on a Blue, Blue Sea

Land in the distance, a shoreline,
shoulders, something to hold onto
when everything else is
unmoored, unlaced,
unhinged; the details are murky,
all fine lines and fingers in my hair,
thick as seaweed, the sun so high and bright
shining on the water,
on our bodies of water,
and people all over the world
crying out, or crying.

Learning to Play Piano at Thirty

Everywhere I lay my hands
I hear music. Each touch
on the computer keyboard,

my fingers drumming
scales on the bedside table
as I'm falling asleep.

I feel my brain unfolding,
gently, like a silk scarf.
I learn to play with two

hands, in minor keys, with feeling.
Alone in my room, I write
a sonata, then an opera.

The house begins to flood,
seams bursting, notes
trickling down the walls.

You still haven't come back,
so I have to do the rescuing myself,
using the piano bench as a raft.

April in Minnesota

The edges of my anger
have been sanded down;
we no longer bump against them
each time we turn
in these crowded rooms.
It's been months since I woke
to thoughts of suicide

(however distant and ill-formed),
and I have stopped blaming you
if the sky is too blue
or not blue enough.

We are hopeful, yet tentative
with each other after these long
winter months, wary of unfinished
corners that might still threaten
to rage forward and split us
when we are already bloodied and raw.

Our neighbor spends each weekend
outdoors now, pushing a mower
past one wall of our house. Inside
his garage, the tools are neatly ordered
on the shelves, every rake and shovel
hanging on its own hook.

Monday comes again.
I wake fearful, not remembering
that the sharp edges of my shoulders
have been rounded,
the clumps of my fists
smoothed into fingers.

Outside our kitchen window,
the sun's anemic early light
falls on grass so green and perfect
that it looks like the set of a play.

All the house is silent,
waiting for my entrance.

At Last, I Am Returned

At last, I am returned
to the dollhouse.

I don't know how long
I've been gone,

but it's such a relief
to be back

in the perfect little house
with its living room sofas

and dining room table set
to serve a feast for six

and the four-poster bed
with its dear little bedspread.

I hold the teacup
in my tiny mitten hands

and can't believe
my good fortune.

In the Driveway, Washing the Car

His mother died lying in bed
watching *Wheel of Fortune*.

He keeps forgetting
that she's dead, keeps picking up

the phone to call her house
and ask if she needs a refill

of her medication or a ride
to the doctor's office.

She'd been ill for so long
that it was as much of a shock

as if she'd been a health nut
in her early thirties.

On Mother's Day, he washes her car
and puts on two coats of wax

just the way she used to like it,
and makes himself a breakfast

of chocolate croissants and bacon
with a pitcher of milk and fresh flowers

on the table. That evening, I see
the blue glow of his television

as he watches all the game shows
he's spent the rest of the week taping.

That evening, as I'm taking off
my macaroni necklaces,

from the window of my bedroom
I can see the blue glow.

Probabilities

There was nowhere to stop back then—
forty-five minutes of scrub brush
and the empty road ahead—
no gas stations, no rest stops,
not even a phone booth to call for help.

One night we drove past
a young woman without a coat
walking by the side of the road
and my parents stopped
to ask if her car had broken down

because that's what people did then,
but she was barefoot and wouldn't
(or couldn't) respond, and so they asked me
to try to convince her to get into the car
with us. It was dark, and cold,

and on the radio Crystal Gayle was singing—
she was on all the country stations then,
a pretty woman with dark hair that fell in a curtain
almost down to her feet. I'd read once
that she had to use an entire bottle of shampoo

every time she washed it, though who knew
if that was true or not. And sometimes
I'm not sure whether these are good memories
or bad—leaning out the car window
trying to coax a stranger to stop walking

and crawl into the back seat with me
though she might have had a knife in her belt
but in the dark she seemed as fragile as a deer
and in this life sometimes you have to choose,
and so they stopped the car and I called her over.

Velocity

And then, suddenly, time is moving too fast.
At the hospital, the magazine has Ben Affleck
vacationing with his girlfriend in Puerto Rico,
but on the internet their breakup is old news:
he's already gone through a Jack in the Box
drive-thru with a Playboy Playmate
and Jennifer Garner checked him back
into rehab. In the chair next to me
a woman is using one finger to scroll through
her Twitter feed like a zombie
while a man across the room stabs impatiently
at the buttons of the coffee machine.
Now Demi Lovato has left Cedars-Sinai
and gone to treatment. It seems that
the missing bodies are finally turning up
and the fall shows are almost ready to debut;
wildfires continue to burn up and down the west coast,
and a twin-engine Cessna carrying five people
crashed into the parking lot of a strip mall
and everyone on board was killed.
We're on the cusp of a drought, a flood,
the quake to end all quakes: the earth is loosening,
careening off its axis, waves convulsing
against the shore. Faster, louder.
All around us, they're sounding the alarms,
and still we go on sitting here. Waiting, waiting.

5150

This time, I get to ride next to her
in the back of the ambulance.

It's a short distance
to the hospital

but the only things they trust now
are the numbers on the form.

They wheel the gurney through
the back hallways of the ER

to finish paperwork and unbuckle
the straps that are holding her down

and set her free.
We are still standing around when

a young man walks into the room
and removes a piece of equipment,

then another man and another item,
until we are surrounded by young men

in scrubs, systematically stripping the room
of every curtain and cord,

and because it's not really necessary
I'm slow to understand what's happening.

She is sitting up on the bed, and when
she looks around and says

that the room is full of blackbirds,
it takes a second to realize

that she's making a joke;
she has emerged from the fog

and is herself again—smart, funny—
making light of the fact that she's now

on a suicide watch and the ER techs
can't leave anything behind;

they pick and pull until nothing is left
but her bed and my chair.

We all laugh but it's uneasy
until everyone else leaves

and it's just the two of us again
(and the security guard, sitting

on a chair in the hallway, just outside the door
that we're not allowed to close).

My husband has gone home
to put the children to bed.

All of us are waiting for the test results
to prove that this isn't a bad trip

or a fever, and then the phone call
that will send her

wherever they can find a bed.
There was a time, during an earlier

hospital stay, when I saw a woman
sitting on a bus bench talking to herself

and I thought, *that could be her
someday.*

I almost couldn't take
the pain I felt then.

Now, curiously, I don't feel anything,
just tired. It makes me think of a long labor:

the hours of waiting, the exhaustion,
the medical tests, the night dragging on so long

that you forget, briefly, and then remember,
all over again, why you are even here.

She was at the clinic early that afternoon,
but it feels like another lifetime.

In the middle of the night, a new guard
brings me a heated blanket.

For months, that moment slips back
into my mind: the feeling of waking up

in the dark, slumped over on a chair inside
the emergency room, and a young man,

a stranger, placing a warm blanket over me.
He said quietly, *you seemed cold,*

and it's true—I was shivering—

and every time I thought that I might die
of grief I thought of him bringing that blanket

as she lay in the hospital bed
next to me, asleep, with a band on her wrist,

and that was the moment I clung to
in the hours until daybreak.

Late May, Botanic Garden, Santa Barbara

I stood in a field of meadowfoam
an ocean of white and yellow wildflowers
while a tourist circled me
with his camera
and the man from the parking lot
who stepped down from a rented pickup truck
in jeans and a plaid button-down and boots
who reached up at the last second
to touch his cowboy hat
uncertainly
has popped open the collar snap of his shirt
and tucked the hat under his arm
his belt buckle shining in the sunlight
in the meadow of yellow flowers
where we will spend all summer
ruffled by the breeze
holding up our faces
in anticipation
of bees
and rain

In the Meadow Next to the Rented House

There was a long road
leading up to the house
we rented that summer.
A brown wooden house
with two stories and rustic
wood siding and darker brown
wood shingles on the roof.

On one side of the gravel drive
was the tall brown house
and on the other side
was a wide meadow
and a pair of horses
separated from us
by a delicate wire fence.

The meadow was dotted
with little yellow wildflowers
as if it were a picture
postcard we intended
to send back to our families.
You washed carrots
and went outside.

But which story will this be?
Soft lighting, wind chimes
hung from the eaves,
the suggestion of wild mint
growing along the fence?
Or will the horse turn its head
and bruise or even break the skin?

Inside, the peels are
in the sink. The sun's head
is heavy, falling slowly toward
the ground. Still, you think you hear
chimes, see a hint of green.
Walk forward.
Hold out your hand.

About the Author

Leah Browning is the author of *Two Good Ears* and *Loud Snow*, mini-books of flash fiction published by Silent Station Press in 2021 and 2022. She is also the author of three short nonfiction books and six chapbooks of poetry and fiction. Browning's work has previously appeared in *Harpur Palate, Four Way Review, Valparaiso Fiction Review, The Threepenny Review, Flock, Necessary Fiction, Watershed Review, Parhelion Literary Magazine, Newfound, The Forge Literary Magazine, Random Sample Review, Superstition Review, Santa Ana River Review, The Homestead Review, Thin Air Magazine, Belle Ombre, The Petigru Review, South 85 Journal, Belletrist Magazine, The Ilanot Review, The Big Windows Review, The Broadkill Review, Oyster River Pages, Poetry South, Clementine Unbound, Coldnoon, Tipton Poetry Journal, Scapegoat Review, The Stillwater Review,* and elsewhere. Her work has also appeared on materials from Broadsided Press and Poetry Jumps Off the Shelf, with audio and video recordings in The Poetry Storehouse, and in anthologies including *The Doll Collection* from Terrapin Books and *Nothing to Declare: A Guide to the Flash Sequence* from White Pine Press. In addition to writing, Browning serves as editor of the *Apple Valley Review*. She is originally from New Mexico.

www.ingramcontent.com/pod-product-compliance
Lightning Source LLC
Chambersburg PA
CBHW022147160426
43197CB00009B/1463